Reality of Life

By Mikel Spahi

Reality of Life

Copyright © 2021 by Mikel Spahi

All Rights Reserved. No part of this publication may be reproduced, stored in a retrieval system, or transmitted in any form by any means, electronic, mechanical, photocopy, recording, or otherwise, without the prior permission of the publisher, except as provided by USA copyright law.

Contents

THE PRESIDENT	2
STAND UP WOMAN FOR THE LAST TIME	4
ROSA PARKS	6
A MOTHER'S HEART	9
QUEEN ELIZABETH II	12
A TRUE LEADER	16
EVERY DAY I AM WITH YOU IS NOT A DREAM, IT'S VALENTINE	18
ALL THE PEOPLE	20
MANHATTAN 2001	22
THE POLICE OUR FALLEN ANGELS FROM THE SKY	26
DISSAPOINTED PARENTS	33
THE PROUD	36
YOU HAVE FALLEN IN LOVE	40
MY MOTHER WAS BLACK, SHE WAS NOT A SCHOLAR	42
THE ASTRONAUTS	47
THE HIDDEN CRIME	50
THE CIGARETTE OF MY SOUL	52
SOMEONE	58

THE BEGGAR	60
THE REFUGEE	62
DO I LIVE OR NO?	64
THERE IS NO SERENITY	66
FATE	68
IF	69
A MONOTONOUS DILEMMA	70
THE NIGHT	71
TELL ME IT IS NOT TRUE	73
THE SEA WAVES	75
AIR BREEZE	77
I WANT TO CRY BUT I CANNOT	78
REALITY OF LIFE	79
THE SONGS OF HONOR	81
THE LIAR	83
WHO IS IN FAULT?	84
TO PHILOSOPHY	85
HELLO	88
THE SAILOR	89
HELPING	92
DON'T FORGET	94
THE ANGUISH OF A PURE HEART	96

THE MEMORY AND THE NEW LIFE	97
A TROUBLED SPIRIT	98
AS OF TODAY	100
FAREWELL OLD LIFE	102
THE ROAD	103
THE LEGENDARY HERO	106
TIME TIRED ME	108
THE WRITER	110
WAIT FOR ME	113
YOUTH	114
A HONEST DRINKER	116
DON'T CRY MAN FOR HAPPINESS	120
THE ELDER'S CANE	124
A CHILD CAME IN THE WORLD	127
INJUSTICE	129
I AM WAITING	130
THE PLAY OF LIFE	132
O GREAT GOD	134
I WOULDN'T LEAVE YOU	135
COME TO SEARCH FOR ME	136
INTEREST	138
FOR YOU	141

I WANT TO BE ALSO LIKE YOU	143
THE EMPTY PROMISE	144
YOU DON'T KNOW WHAT GRATITUDE IS	145
SINGLE OR MARRIED	147
LIFE CAN BE TOUGH	149
LET US TREAT EACH OTHER WITH RESPECT AND LOVE AND WE WILL BE JUST FINE	151
GOOD LUCK TO YOU AND GOOD LUCK TO ME	154
BILLIONS OF PEOPLE	156
THE HUMAN NOVEL	157

THE PRESIDENT

All in your eye look
and after your steps go.
You should be proud
because in you we believe.

So it will be the future
for protecting this dear land,
the name "America" not to fade,
and the truth to triumph everywhere.

The history of America will continue,
among centuries this country will reign,
the leaders and the patriots
time itself will honor.

Source:

https://en.wikipedia.org/wiki/File:Mount_Rushmore_detail_view_(100MP).jpg

STAND UP WOMAN FOR THE LAST TIME

How much you have suffered!
How much you have cried!
How many times you have been abused!
How many times to you they have lied!
In how many ways they have tried to break you down,
but you always stood up and got back your crown.

Thousands of years have gone but still
you are facing injustice, discrimination, violence.
Raise your voice because the greatest enemy is silence.
They want to control your body, your freedom, your life
but you are nobody's property.
So stand up again women, show as always your bravery.

Every time they try to put you down, stand up again,
cause your strength and love is greater than your pain.
Stand up woman for the last time
because only you can carry the world in shoulders.
This world that is for everyone
yours and mine.

ROSA PARKS

Now when I get on the bus
a feeling of love caresses me.
I don't know what appeals
but a noble woman it reminds me.

I sit, look around
and say, "in our hearts
you are alive."

You gave courage to people,
you gave future
to peace and love.

You did not put the umbrella
amid the rain and storm,
but stood strong in your beliefs
and opened way to justice.

Now you smile
when you see us united.
You should know
that the name "Rosa Parks"
will never be forgotten.

Source: https://www.albawaba.com/editors-choice/handwritten-letter-rosa-parks-martin-luther-king-sale-54000-1372477

A MOTHER'S HEART

You went beyond the sea
together with the wind,
you couldn't greet even the spring.
You went with joy and left me.
All night I think
and sleep doesn't seize me.

You left with a fulminant walk
in a foreign city,
while I, desolate,
in this land am suffering.

You left, forgot me, without saying why
but remember well
whose son you are.

Source: https://homeschooladventure.com/blog/okay-to-dream-good-wife-mother/

Source: https://en.wikipedia.org/wiki/Elizabeth_II

QUEEN ELIZABETH II

Now most of young women on their 20s
are making only selfies, partying,
drinking vodka and gin.
But you on that age started to serve your people
and became a Glorious Queen.
With your beautiful smile
and bright eyes,
words of wisdom when you spoke,
made even philosophers to think twice.

In difficult times of war
when everything seemed to be falling apart,
your courage and support
gave people hope
and made them to fight with
a lion's heart.

How many events have your seen?
In how many places have you been?
You always fought for justice and peace,
you wanted the best for humanity.
You did what you could within your power,
but changing this world for good
needs the participation of all people,
because summer doesn't come only
with one flower.

Here you are today after many years have gone,
standing proud with your crown
in the well-deserved throne.
You don't have to say a word
even your silence is understood.
Just your presence in this world
makes us feel very good.
As high as the mountains,
as deep as the oceans,
with your great personality
we love you, your Majesty.

And we wish you always happiness,
long life and all the best,
to you and the royal family.

This world has billions of people,
they can say whatever they want,
they can do whatever they want to do,
but one thing is for certain
that there will never be a QUEEN like YOU.

A TRUE LEADER

To be a leader
is not easy indeed.
It is not a job where one can sleep.
Where there is chaos, you have to find peace,
where there is night,
you have to make light.
The heart of people you will gain
not by empty promises
and lying without shame,
but walking in truth
having integrity even in pain.
Some will say go right
and some will say go left,

you have to have the compass within you
to follow the path of your star,
to see through clouds that are near or far.
To be a leader is not easy indeed,
it is not about fame and glory
but service to all,
with wisdom and love,
humility to know when to listen,
the courage to march forward
when all want to retreat without a thought.
A true leader is a lighthouse
amid storms and turbulent waves,
giving hope to future,
strengthening the weak and guiding the braves.

EVERY DAY I AM WITH YOU IS NOT A DREAM, IT'S VALENTINE

There are many lovers out there
but like you and I are rare.
In my mind I think only for you
and in my heart only for you I care
I don't want expensive holidays at the beach,
I don't want any yachts or a private plane,
I am the richest one every time you call my name.

I don't want a castle neither a diamond ring
our mutual respect and understanding
is enough every year
from summer until spring.

Couples don't need to travel the world to be happy
cause happiness is in the heart and mind,
if true love like us everyone can find.
Today is February 14^{th,}
I found in my room flowers, chocolates, and wine,
but today I want to tell you something darling,
you always make me laugh, with you I feel great all the time.
Even if you don't buy me anything is fine,
this day is not any special from other days,
cause every day I am with you
it is not a dream, it is Valentine.

ALL THE PEOPLE

They walk in full elegance
Have you seen how they look?
All proud
the unknown seek.

O! How beautiful they smile
my heart gets filled with joy,
O! With how much pain they cry
my bread becomes sadness.

O! How good they talk
how I like to imitate.
Why don't they go toward peace,
this I don't understand.

O! How beautiful life separates
and again it joins.
Jew, Christian, and Muslim
the same earth circles us.

All of us are people
but the example of humanity
for a peaceful world
is every good and just human.

MANHATTAN 2001

The day of September 11th
worldwide emotion.
In that sky without boundary
terrorism got its head out,
even the sun blackened
when all the city shook.

The big cloud with rancor
hit it straight in the heart
and all the earth appalled.

Thus were fading two torches
from the highest to the first floor.
They tried to survive
but fatal wounds they had taken.

Thousands of stars were killed
and thousands of sounds were heard,
then weary
on Manhattan's land they fell.

Stand up people!
We must protect
firmly the democracy.

Listen well
and don't look confused,
the criminals and the unjust
must be fought.

President Bush himself declared,
"Democracy will never fade."
This hurtful event
let history write.

Source:

https://www.news18.com/photogallery/world/18-years-since-911-attacks-the-101-most-iconic-photos-805219.html

THE POLICE OUR FALLEN ANGELS FROM THE SKY

24 hours on duty

in snow heat and rain

you put your lives at risk,

and yet they offend and disrespect you

without any shame.

On any emergency you and the ambulance

are the first to be there

not even their own mother.

But for doing your job trying to save lives

still some people see you as a bother.

You are the ones who really ensure law and order.
In this chaotic world full of disorder
you are the lights of the city.
Without you catching the bad guys
our neighborhoods wouldn't look so pretty.
Remember as long as you do your job as you should
you are the king of the throne,
but if you cross the red line
the power and respect for you is gone.
So make sure you stay on track
or put your hands behind your back.

There is no room for you to do injustice,
you are not like the rest.
All eyes and trust are on you
and you should stay as you are, always the best.
If a police officer breaks the law, everyone protests,
willing to burn and fight everywhere.
But when police officers die on duty
some people stay silent like they don't care.
To all of you who want to defund the police
go find another country to live please,
or maybe go live in a jungle
so you can do whatever you want.

Steal, fight, shoot, kill
with no police or anyone to bother.
If you want, go ahead and share your neighborhood
with a lion, hyena, or a tiger as your sister and brother

Instead of asking to defund the police
teach your kids and your husbands
not to steal, not to kill, not to cause any trouble,
or make someone a cripple.
With the situation that is present right now
police should double and even triple.
Police exist because on the same problems we stumble,
a few uncivilized people from any race,
white, red, yellow, black, and brown
don't know what respect, integrity, and love is.

They don't know how to solve their problems
in civilized manner in court,
instead they want to turn everything upside down.
Many people are violent, they don't know
how to solve their problems in peace,
so that's why we need the police.
Police are often under lots of stress,
on one side they have to deal with bad guys
and on the other side with a corrupt
justice system that is more of a mess.
Lawmakers have allowed citizens
to buy and sell guns like a money exchanger,
putting the lives of police officers
and everyone else even more in danger.

That's why the police must be separated
from the government because
they exist not only to arrest wrongdoing civilians
but everyone who breaks the law,
starting from colleagues to their brother,
to judges, prosecutors, senators, lawmakers,
the sheriff, the mayor, the governor, the president,
even their own wife, kids, and mother,
because nobody has the right to harm or
destroy other people's lives.
Police have taken an oath to uphold the law,
not to be friends with corrupt evil people
or to run a TV show.

Being a police officer is the most noble job
that can ever be,
if you work with the highest integrity.

Police officers should get the highest salary.
You are not our enemy,
you are our brothers and sisters, our family.
We love you and respect you,
so hold your shiny badges high,
cause you are our real heroes,
our fallen angels from the sky.

DISSAPOINTED PARENTS

O parents, you work every day, exhausted
for you have children to raise.
With love you clothe them, feed them
and hope that when you grow old,
from them a little comfort to find.
You become stressed, troubled, sighing,
and often time you laugh and cry.
With life every day you fight
so you can give to your children more,
to educated them and make them happy.

And so after all those years
old age catches you.
Even though you are wrinkled, grey-haired, unable,
love for your children becomes greater.
But they get married, go away, and you parents
become lonely.
Their justification is that, "We are young,
we will go out, we will be happy. You can
stay with no worries for we will remember."
As far as you are still able to move,
even though old
your children still take advantage of you.
They give you to raise your grandchildren
for the youth have no time, they will work.

Finally, when the day comes
that your petals wither like that of a rose,
even though you wait for your dear children
to at least give you a glass of water,
they plan to send you in asylum.

THE PROUD

Everywhere they go
they undervalue you
and themselves they raise up.
I am an engineer,
I build apartments without a sweat.
I am a pilot,
I fly the plane without hands.

"While I," says the cleaner,
"have a daughter who is a doctor."
"While I ," says the shoemaker,
have a wife who is a director."

"While I," says a carpenter,
"my son is finishing for a lawyer
in his special field."
"While I," says a painter,
"my son works as a coordinator,
while my daughter has all As and will be a judge."

"And I," says an economist, "when I count the money
my eyes hurt because they can't be numbered."
"I am sorry for interrupting," says a lady,
"but I also want to introduce myself.
I am a teacher of language and literature
and my husband I married with love."

"Slow down," says a villager, "you married with love while I married as quick as you close and open your eyes."

"While we," said the priest and the mufti,
"collect the money
from people in churches and mosques
and even though we don't give any money
to the poor beggars,
or pray just for show,
we still praise ourselves saying that we are saintly
because we do good deed as God has ordered."

      Oh with these people,

      you ask how they are

and not want jobs they do or who they are,

   while their mind is only to brag.

YOU HAVE FALLEN IN LOVE

Your mind has left you
who knows where it flies,
and you remain as confused
every time you start to think.
Sometimes you laugh with yourself
and sleep doesn't come,
but even when it comes
you sleep with open eyes.

These recent times you have started
to look at the mirror more,
even your eyes look with a different color.
"Father," you said one day
and you became quiet again.
There is no need to speak
for I know dear daughter,
you have fallen in love.

MY MOTHER WAS BLACK, SHE WAS NOT A SCHOLAR

When I was born, all nurses
came around.
Some of them left the room
others said to my mother,
"What a cute boy Mrs. Jackson.
Congratulations, you should be proud."
My mother smiled
and then she started crying.
Hundreds of thoughts
in her mind were flying.
"Stop crying," said the doctor, "enough,
everything will be all right."

"Thank you Doc," said my mother,
" you know life for
people like us with dark skin is very tough."
"I know," said the doctor, "but don't let you child
on the streets.
Teach him always to be kind, to love, and to be the best
then don't worry for the rest.
The world has not yet fallen apart
same as there are racist people
who discriminate us based on our color,
there are also millions of others
who judge based on our behavior and our heart."
Then her eyes were filled with light
as she held me tight.

When I grew up
my mother taught me how to be a good man,
how not to hurt anyone, how not to lie,
but to always help people.
To say good morning instead of goodbye.
My mother taught me everything.
How not to use people as bait,
how not to discriminate.
She taught me to forgive,
live and let live,
but she never taught me history,
filled with terrible events and slavery.

She said, "I want you to be in peace my son,
not to be racist or hate anyone.
Forget about what people say,
don't compare yourself with anyone,
try to be always better than you were yesterday.
With your good behavior make all racist people
to feel guilty of who they are.
Make everyone to want to be like you
shining like a star."
There are many mothers out there
rich and famous, even with PHD,
but all of their kids want to be like me.
My mother was black,
she was not a scholar
but she taught me one thing:
to treat everyone with respect,
as my sister and brother.

Maybe I'm poor and with no degree
but everyone wants to be like me.
My mother was black,
she was not a scholar,
but I'm proud of her
because she taught me how to be a real human being,
with humanistic values.
And I wouldn't change who I am
even if you gave me a billion dollars.

My mother was black,
she was not a scholar.

THE ASTRONAUTS

I take in my hands physics,
and then chemistry
a melancholic voice says,
"remember the tragedy."
My hands tremble
my eyes drop tears
those tragic moments
I can't believe.
From the wide space
in the unending horizon,
seven stars were descending
with longing and love.

Their families waiting with
anguish and emotions,
suddenly are heart-pierced
with news of explosion.
But though saddened,
let's pray for these heroes
of the Earth,
for these braves of the world.

In year 2005 the poem "The Astronauts" was chosen and won a prize in the competition of "International Poetry" and it was published in their book "The Colors of Life."

Source:

https://en.wikipedia.org/wiki/File:Space_Shuttle_Columbia_launching.jpg

THE HIDDEN CRIME

How much I wanted to be
in the shore of the sea
and to keep with all the strength that I had
the waves of the earthquake.

Those waves who took
thousands of lives,
those waves who did
a hidden crime.

And let nature
vent its fury in me,
after, let its face laugh
as much as it wanted.

Many people died,
others remained
with no bread, no house,
but the criminal no one could catch.

All the world was astounded,
saw you in wonder,
an innocent crime you did.

THE CIGARETTE OF MY SOUL

The siren of the police
is being heard again,
the sky's clouds
are pouring rain.

The bell of the church
is chiming again.

And there, a little farther
a building that was
now has changed,
has turned in a museum.

      Pain is passing
      through my body.
  Where did the friendship go?
Why have I been left an orphan?

   When the stars see me
     they suspire,
they go farther to ask Heaven.

Is the middle of the night,
   fog without turn,
   the streets betray,
where to go, I don't know.

The cigarette that I smoke
is comforting,
its fume
my lungs is petting.

Thousands of sounds go
thousands of sounds come,
life is not a dance
but simply a mandolin.

Our ancestors were truly good,
ashamed be the one who laughs in darkness.

You take pleasure when others
you destroy.
Rise people!
Quickly change!

When you have the railroad
why do you go to the wagon?

The siren of the police
justice seeks.
Hundreds of persons
without facts are accused.

With my tear
I am blowing out this cigarette
otherwise its smoke
is going to make me sick.

Source: https://freepolicybriefs.org/2011/09/19/do-russians-oppose-anti-tobacco-policy/

SOMEONE

Someone knows what love is
another doesn't know what it is.

Someone stays behind shackles
for what he has done,
another fills fists of sand.

Someone follows
the laws of the state,
another guards the king's cup.

    Someone is hurt in the soul
for what was done to him in perfidy.

        Another looked
          toward God,
        God gave him light,
        man's tear was dried.

THE BEGGAR

In the wet earth a beggar lay
his eyes laughed in the livid body.

He saw me with the head down, like numb,
tried to open his frozen hand,
sought to speak but his voice was gone.

An unusual light flashed at him,
I approached; he was melting like a candle.

An abstract death
petted him strangely.
Even the sky cried with nostalgia
because this torch that faded was
"The Beggar."

Source:

https://strangerwall.wordpress.com/2015/07/15/random-thoughts-how-the-beggars-are-well-modernized-in-terms-of-begging-by-ellie/

THE REFUGEE

Such a gloomy day has been today,
everything is filled full of tears.
Somebody very far away is migrating,
mother, home is remembering.

Passing the mountains one by one
and finally arriving in a foreign land.

Trouble has caught you o forlorn,
you eat some bread with jam
but no, you can't swallow that morsel.

Round and round you are looking
while where will you work
you think.

With the head down
a hardest job you look for.

You are very right to be silent
though your soul groans.
O you poor refugee,
who drag day and night.

Thus, for a better life
you search the lighter in the dark.

DO I LIVE OR NO?

Since I was born,
I looked toward the sun
its rays and the sky's clouds.

I began to grow up little by little
going toward life
every day by a step.

I played, talked
with bad and good,
drank brandy
and often even beer.

The years were passing
and the age got old,
and I was evening
like that lonely oak.
Then, in the elder's age
I drank coffee.

It flashed one day
in my head
and I started to read.
Suddenly I asked myself:
"Do I live or no?"

THERE IS NO SERENITY

Now it is raining,
the sun has become muddy,
the sky blackened.

Rattles the mountain from lightening,
is filled the world
all with mines,
everywhere smoke and cars.

Even if you are in a high position
in peace they don't leave you,
they follow you back with money
like the old man that drinks coffee.

Fall o! rain without cease,
drown everything with impatience.
Make the cliffs dissolved
because people should have serenity
to live in happiness.

FATE

Two ways God gives;
one askew
and one toward justice.

But fate is what we choose
ourselves,
therefore we should not curse
the sky and the clouds.

IF

If I went there, outside,
and talked nonsense,
at once friends would come
to applaud me for my words.

If I was not clever
they would make me as a brother.
If I spied for others
they would give me
beer and wine.

But like this I cannot act
that's why "if" is a useless word.

A MONOTONOUS DILEMMA

With a wet heart,
sinking in pessimism
I see things in the same prism.

Wet from the furious rain
I have left the windows and the doors.
The doors for getting in
and the windows for looking out.

I will sing always for life
with an old friend called guitar.

THE NIGHT

Oh you splendid night
together with the moon
as an ice cream,
that brightens all the world
from one side to the other!

And the stars all around,
with prettiness how they shine,
to the hopeless traveler
the heart they delight.

Stay o! night a little longer,
that I see this wonder.
The tearful eyes of people
let them fill with love.

Source:https://www.pinterest.es/pin/241505598753577902/?amp_client_id=CLIENT_ID(_)&mweb_unauth_id={{default.session}}&from_amp_pin_page=true

TELL ME IT IS NOT TRUE

Dried, numb, drunken, frozen
I have come to tell you goodbye.
In real darkness you banished me
you gave me wine and brandy.

From my head smoke and fire I give off
every word amongst you bewildered I listen.

You didn't let a place without digging,
look to yourselves, you damn cursed.
Nonsense words coming out of your mouth.

    The good, the bad,
    the fed-up, the greedy,
    the honest, thieves,
    the quiet, the lout,
    they became all the same.

It seems like in a dream I am living,
    get out of my sight reality
    tell me that it is not true.

THE SEA WAVES

Go, you waves of the sea, go
another seashore to seek.
Go with fury,
go like crazy
and guzzle what you find ahead.

The wind with you will whistle,
flying will grab you.

Go thus, o! waves of the sea
and the dusk of this night
leave to the city.

Source:
https://www.pinterest.com/pin/7599893101035675/

AIR BREEZE

A breeze of air fondles me,
I want to stay
but the dust doesn't delay.

Another breeze of air
fondles me,
I want to go
but my heart it troubles.

Blows the air breeze in my hair,
I stay silent
and look towards heaven.

I WANT TO CRY BUT I CANNOT

I want to cry but I have no tears,
forlorn me that cannot bear.
I want to cry
for you unfortunate.
You think that I laugh
but in my soul
I have an abyss.

How this world has changed
from Adam's time till today!
I want to cry people
but I cannot,
for I would fill
an ocean with tears.

REALITY OF LIFE

Look how I creep,
I, the sinful snake,
I twist and roll
like a rope.

I seize all the roads,
with the owl's eye I see,
behind the world's doors
silently I peek.

I am here amongst you
and enjoy myself in this world,
I eat and have eaten the grapes
around the world.

Always, everywhere in life,
I have come out the first,
so the righteous lose,
the tricky win.

I don't understand
how they don't understand,
why straight to evil
hastily they go.

In the white snow
there are many black spots.
Trickery, lies,
but even the truth
are gathered all of them by this life.

THE SONGS OF HONOR

They were written from pain
and with pride.
They were not only words,
but had a living beauty.
They were written for soldiers,
heroes, and patriots.
And where did they have the power
to keep people always in bosom?
Every time I hear them
I love to sing,
for they make me want to live.

They melt amongst us
as grains of sugar.
They will always remain golden
because they are songs of honor.

In year 2006 the poem "The Songs of Honor" was chosen and won a prize in the competition of the publishers "Noble House" and it was published in their book "The Songs of Honour."

THE LIAR

I have seen you almost never,
maybe you forgot me forever.
You promised me everyday
but you didn't keep your word.

You promised me a lot
from summer until spring.
So better let's turn off this fire
for you are only a liar.

WHO IS IN FAULT?

The earth has fault
but they saw heaven.
The moon spied
but they told the sun.

The clouds dropped the rain,
they went to the sea.
From the wind
the weather got bad,
people went to God.

Who has fault
no one knows,
without concrete facts
don't accuse anyone.

TO PHILOSOPHY

With the unbending spirit
of a warrior,
with the wounded heart
of a father.

When scent
brings you to the gold
with the mastery of a dab,
the instinct of desires
fuddle you so good,
your mind gets lost
among the darkness.

    This magic dust
that has spread in the world,
where different people
all life are consuming.

The philosophical progress
as a thread,
how limited is the Reminiscence,
unseen often becomes the existence.

If we all philosophy so much
everything would seem like in a sleep.

Source: https://www.thoughtco.com/profile-of-socrates-121053

HELLO

Let's leave aside the vanities,
bring in here the beers brother.
Let's drink a whole sea,
we must make our belly wide.

No, what are you? And what am I?
With these things
we can't win any deed.
Let's drink until one o'clock
that we fight never more.

How far away is
for you the truth,
but let's say better a "hello".

THE SAILOR

It was a bad weather.
Rain was falling.
The ship was pushed by a storm.
He alone with his heart,
gave courage to himself,
gave to the ship strength.

The wave wanted to bring him down
but he didn't give up.
Thunder wanted to burn him
but he was not afraid.

He faced nature
and stood proud.
Nothing defeated
this son of men.
His name was sailor.

Source: https://www.publicdomainpictures.net/en/view-image.php?image=313417&picture=sailor-grave

HELPING

Many people help ask
but many don't understand.
Helping is not riches
is not a hand or a helmet.

Helping is a humane sign
it is the true teller.

When someone asks for something
it is enough to say the good word,
don't give any bread or money.

Source:

https://www.publicdomainpictures.net/en/hledej.php?hleda=helping

DON'T FORGET

Don't wipe from yourself
the mistake you made.
Lift your eyes up
toward the shining stars.

Sincere faces
before you pass,
your eyes
unclean tears will drop.

You try to hide yourself every day,
but you cannot hold
with a paper the storms.

Now you can do anything
but the mistake you made
don't forget.

THE ANGUISH OF A PURE HEART

How much I want to enclose in eternity,
to cry and scream with fury.
To go away from this enchanted world
and stay for a little time in solitude.

Every time my eyes I forcibly press
many kinds of creatures I recall.

The rich, the poor, the happy,
the loner, the raiders, the flatterers,
evil voices of youth,
crows and ravens of the sky.

This anguish for how long will continue
or perhaps for centuries will reign?

THE MEMORY AND THE NEW LIFE

I follow now the waves of the sea,
leaving behind all the commotion.
I follow it with passion and with wonder,
feeling still shaken.

I follow this wave of my new life.
I ask where it goes but it doesn't tell.
The sea wants to make me a surprise
and this makes me follow it like a spear.

A TROUBLED SPIRIT

Sometimes everything seems empty
the same things year after year.
The daily monotony
doesn't want to part,
it has become like inedible bread.

Who are we? Where we come from?
From the earth or the white clouds?

Thousands of moans
follow these troubled spirits,
thousands of thoughts
make us as bewildered.

This New Year is coming,
maybe the way of living
will change surprisingly.

Maybe we will learn
what the meaning of "human" is,
maybe we will live in more harmony.

AS OF TODAY

Today I have left my house,
for me the history changed.

If you knew how much I have suffered,
Mountains, fields, I have passed by
from my homeland I have gone away.

Across the skies and over the clouds
no one asked, "How are you?"

Without eating, without drinking
I have done a difficult road.

Thus as of today
I have come to my family,
I have found a treasure.

But tomorrow how is it going to be?
A dream or the truth.

FAREWELL OLD LIFE

Farewell old life,
farewell childhood.
I didn't want to part like this
but the new life
gave me more responsibility.

Farewell darkness,
farewell o! friend, o! brother,
farewell my dreams,
like a new life, no, there is nothing.

Farewell mother mine,
tomorrow is another day.
With joy in my lips
I am saying farewell to the old life.

THE ROAD

The road has lots of goods,
it has snow and it has rain.
Sometimes it has even storms
from Monday until Saturday.

What can I say,
what doesn't the road have?
In the road people do business,
there you find work
and you find a house.

The road is with no limit
in earth as well as space.
It makes you white or black.

The road has even danger,
so you have to know
how to walk my friends.

Source: http://onebigphoto.com/green-road/

THE LEGENDARY HERO

I am sorry people
that I came in this world.
Forgive me people
for I am full of mercy.

I am the traveler of my ancestors,
I am the one who remembers them
with nostalgia.
I am the forgotten human.
I don't recognize here amongst you
the word "love".

People, don't try

the thoughts from the soul to command,

for it would take centuries

until you understand.

TIME TIRED ME

I loved people a lot surprisingly
but time tired me perfidiously,
perhaps it didn't want
that I live meanly.

I asked it to give me more strength
but God himself didn't want to.
It was written
I would not be left in bleakness.

I tried to speak to people
year after year
but all this try was in vain,
like them I couldn't do.

My eyes laughed from the tears
and I washed them in a fountain.
But suddenly an angel approached
and said, "Come with me,
for only God and I love you."

THE WRITER

I am sitting here in the library,
someone studies, another rests.
I lift my head high and see
thousands of books, unending.
Then I smile to myself in secrecy,
"All these I can't read."

I take in my hands
a book of poetry,
the poems of author X I read
but his name I couldn't discover.

The writer is a scientist
of life and literature,
for this mystery there is no explanation,
this is a gift of God.

Source: https://www.telegraph.co.uk/only-in-britain/percy-bysshe-shelley-born/

WAIT FOR ME

Runs time,
but for me doesn't wait.
I try to reach it
but hundreds of nights pass.

Runs time in snow, in rain.
I follow but it doesn't stay.
I followed time
but I couldn't catch it.
I grew up fast.

Now I will make time to say,
"Wait for me",
for to follow it in vain
I don't want to anymore.

YOUTH

Today in the age of youth
the cigarette I have started.
Today in the age of twenty
smoke and drugs my life has become.

With these hands
night and day I have worked,
cigarettes and drugs I have bought.
With what I have earned
in gambling I have gone.
And what did I win?

Thus as of today and nevermore,
youth I tell you this thing:
Change your ways and behave
so that a glass of water
when you drink
will seem like a beer.

A HONEST DRINKER

He was stuck one day
in a road with hurdles.
A tall man with mustache
kept a packet in his hand
from an unforgotten pain.

He stayed and watched in a window
smoked ceaselessly his cigarettes.

From the hot sun
his head was boiling,
while for the world's evil
he was thinking.

Life had gifted him
many difficulties
and he had passed them with honesty.

His soul was burning
and he drank brandy.
In the road with thorns
he sat and laid down.

Suddenly he felt dizzy
but he got up,
though in the frail earth he crawled.
"No, No," he said to himself,
I don't want to look as a street's dog".

But his heart was turning
in that of a loner.

Suddenly his lips blackened,
like a willow the reef raised,
and he clashed down again
like a sailor's ship
clashes with cliffs.

The sky flared
and the volcano spilled out rain,
he cringed a little scared.

He tried to get up but he couldn't,
his eyes were filled full of tears.
He tried to get up but again fell,
then with all the strength he had, said,
"Indeed troubles have made me a drunk
but I am honest though."

DON'T CRY MAN FOR HAPPINESS

Don't cry man for happiness
God gifted you solitude.
Melancholy won you over,
for God himself granted it to you.

With heavy steps
you walk,
so many times in nostalgia
the past you remember.

With wet hands
toward a door you knock.
It looks like an illusion
but it is true.

Since no one waits for you,
you are forced to open the door yourself.

And suddenly before you
the stars appear as in a night,
smiles your face
of a deep thinker.

Perhaps beyond those stars
is a better life,
perhaps, but doesn't look so
for there is more darkness.

No, No, I am very glad
to be in solitude,
when I get inspired I write poems.

Though often times
I stand in dilemma,
I pass it reading any fables
or maybe a poem.

What a poor life!
What an unworthy life!
For me loneliness
is winning this time.

Don't cry man for happiness
God gifted you solitude.

THE ELDER'S CANE

Sitting in a chair
under the fog of fate,
I sit and watch the stars
like the lights of flats.

Time for me
now has passed by,
and people how far have gone.
I have been left alone
in this forgotten house.

This wrinkled cane
did not betray,
in every problem I had
it raised and comforted me.

How long do I have to wait?
How long, tell me?
Or crouched like this
as a snail will I suffer?

When it is raining and snowing
I stay near the fire,
but my body doesn't get warm
from the thoughts of a loner.

My daughter in law and son left,
they didn't ask anymore for me.
They said without a waiver in their voice,
"Father we don't love you anymore."

Praise be to almighty God,
if it was for others I would have been gone.

Now I have a question elder's cane:
Tell me where stands in here
the essence of magic?

A CHILD CAME IN THE WORLD

A new child came in this world,
is going to grow amongst us
with smiles and tears.

Now will be known
simply as a child,
but tomorrow we don't know
after him what will come.

From a child comes a lawyer,
from a child comes a scientist,
from a child comes a disturber.
From a child a world is led,
from a child who becomes a man
and never says empty words.

Many children change history,
and each of them
represents humanity.
But who is a human?
A being magnificent,
or a living brain?

We all are people
and if we live in peace,
in that moment God might
bless humanity.

INJUSTICE

Shame on you who play,
shame on you
for transfiguring the laws.
You laugh when you see me suffering
and walk away with no mercy.
For me justice is near
while you keep it away
and with darkness you cover it.

Shame on you for never believing.
Shame on you for denying the truth.

I AM WAITING

Why did you let me suffer,
among the unending rain?
Why didn't you tell me before
what was my name?

Among all this storm
an umbrella keeps me,
everyday I pass
in the same volcano.

I am so tired
from vain words.
Is it possible
for the world to change ?

With my feet on earth
the umbrella I grasp
and wait in anguish
to pass the day.

I hope tomorrow
to get me out of trouble.
I want to help all humanity
then sit in the chair of justice.

So go the hours of my fate
among the boundless sky,
in waiting with no end.

THE PLAY OF LIFE

You seek to play with me,
you have gotten me in a world
that doesn't change.
The day and night
comes and goes,
and you always say,
"Hey, boy, time is going by!"

I know this is
the same day and night
but people don't understand,
while you don't make commotion.

Transformation happens
with me and nature,
but day and night
didn't change their face.

It is a beautiful game
but no one understands.
We yell, stay, and laugh,
the world our mind circles.

Now, I understood the lying game
so I won't play at all.

O GREAT GOD

O Great God,
you created the earth and the heaven.
You own everything, you have great power.
Have you seen people today
they confuse you until you can't get out.

O Great God, have a little mercy
for people who think straight
standing up and lying down.
This world has good people
who suffer and toil from this darkness.

Tell me God because I cannot bear
I am just and no one stops me.
Is there a judge better than you?

I WOULDN'T LEAVE YOU

One day I took a ship
and went in the sea.
I am not a captain
but troubles themselves make you captain.
With this ship I passed many waves
that raised suddenly.
To tell the truth I was also afraid
because I was never trained.
After all that we passed,
there, another storm was coming
but now I was not afraid,
I wouldn't leave you,
I wouldn't leave you.

COME TO SEARCH FOR ME

Don't let me suffer, to cry with tears.
Don't let me shout, for I cannot bear.
Where are you for me?
Tell me how much you love me?
Come to me, come look for me.
These drops of crystal that are falling
don't forget are my tears.
And in those tears
my love remained.
Oh poor heart
how much you have tired.

Amid the deepest distances

of the soul

if you want support

sincerity, and love,

you cannot find it.

Thus do not have shame,

please come, look for me.

INTEREST

When the rose's petals fall.
we say that it is ruined.
When human loses his logic
we call him without value.

When personal interest are touched
we lose love.
We ruin every kind of tie
and forget the friendship.

When someone makes us laugh
we bring him nearer.
When someone makes us cry
we avoid him.

When someone makes us laugh
we bring him nearer.
When someone makes us cry
we avoid him.

When no one gives us, we offend them.
When they give us, we praise them.
All the injustice we accept
the truths we deny.
When a lot of rain falls
we curse the sky.
When the earth dries from heat
we curse the sun.

You want things to go
Always according to your desires
And no one from you says
"With interest I don't want."

FOR YOU

For you I would pass
the highest mountain.
For you I would sail
many months without a map.
For you I would sacrifice
what is most dear for me
only to tell you
how much I love you.

I would not want to remain without you
for nothing beautiful and dear
in this world attracts me.

I am sorry if I don't know
how to love you.
But deep in my soul
you will be with me.

I WANT TO BE ALSO LIKE YOU

Today I threw away the keys of the car
when I saw someone running
amid the rain, exhausted,
because I wanted to run with you.
You became drenched in the sudden rain.

Today I spread all wealth
when I saw a beggar asking,
because I also wanted to feel poor
or from the unconscientious passer- byes
unvalued.
O people when I see you suffering
with tears in those eyes
I also want to be like you.

THE EMPTY PROMISE

Tomorrow and not today
and two days have gone
Tomorrow and not today
and one week has gone.
Tomorrow and not today
and one year has gone.
Tomorrow and not today
and many years have gone.
Don't tell me anymore tomorrow
but say today or never.
Because the man becomes old
and the child, man.

YOU DON'T KNOW WHAT GRATITUDE IS

I took you out of darkness,
I brought you into light,
I taught you to be peaceful
and for true justice to always fight.
I took you out of poverty,
I taught you how to be rich,
I taught you to tell always the truth
and check your own actions before you preach.
I taught you to choose friends based on their personality
not based on their power or money.
There are many strong and big animals out there
but only bees produce honey.

I taught you why from all who say they love you
from your friends, husband, wife, kids, sister or brother,
there is no greater love in this world
than the love of GOD and that of your mother.
I taught you how to be a human and the meaning of life,
with my teachings now you are a gem cutter,
you can face any difficulties without falter.
I taught you many things, but you haven't understood,
even if someone gives you the whole world,
for you that is never enough,
so let us part here please
because you don' know what gratitude is.

SINGLE OR MARRIED

Some people are married.
Some people are single.
Some like to be always in pairs,
others don't want to mingle.
Some like to argue, go shopping, and fight,
and then to laugh and make love at night.
Some like to stay alone
and have a peace of mind.
Someone can't sleep hearing their partner
snoring with delight,
someone else sleeps like a queen
under the moon and stars shining bright.

Most single people want to get married,
some unhappy married couples
wish they were single like before.
Some say out loud, "Oh God I can't take it anymore."
Getting married or staying single is like gambling,
you don't know in the long run
if you will be happy or sad.
So think well before you decide
because happiness is the most important
if you really understand.

LIFE CAN BE TOUGH

I was sitting in the tram
coming back from school to home,
suddenly my eyes caught someone crying
and this hit me like a stone.
Her tears were flowing like rain,
even though she didn`t notice,
deep in my heart I felt her pain.
In that moment nothing would take
my sadness away.

If they would offer me a whole New York City,
still, I wouldn't care.
It`s true we breathe the same air
but same feelings we don`t share.

I couldn't sleep that night
the moon wasn't anymore bright.

For many people life is fun and can be easy enough,
but for people with deep understanding and love
life can be tough, it can be tough.

LET US TREAT EACH OTHER WITH RESPECT AND LOVE AND WE WILL BE JUST FINE

Hey you, this seat is mine
sit on the other seat, you will be just fine.
Hey you, this job in mine
find another one and you will be just fine.
Hey you, this money is mine
work as a slave and you will be just fine.
Hey you, this land is mine
only a room for you will be just fine.
Hey you, I am the major, the sheriff, the judge
and this city is mine,
do what I tell you to do, pay taxes
and you will be just fine

Hey you, this country is mine
go to another country and you will be just fine.
Hey you, this plane is mine
travel with the donkey and you will be just fine.

Hey you, even though I don't have a clue
I voted for someone,
follow my choice and you will be just fine.
Hey you, this place of leadership is mine
I might be incompetent, liar, corrupted
but with me you will be just fine.
Hey you, this world is all mine
find another planet and you will be just fine.

I beg your pardon ladies and gentlemen
but nothing is yours,
most of you just found open doors.

But thank God that I am not your president or the king
because my justice would fall on earth
like rivers in the spring,
and I would have made all of you to say out loud:
"Hey you, this is yours not mine,
this world and universe belong only to GOD,
Let us treat each other with respect and love
and we will be just fine."

GOOD LUCK TO YOU AND GOOD LUCK TO ME

He says, "I love you," in the morning light,
He says, "I miss you," during the day,
He says, "Let's spend together all Saturday night,
and on Sunday let us pray."
I just laugh and I reply:
"I know you love me, and I love you too as a friend,
but I have work and other things to do,
and this you must understand.
Plus you don't share my personality,
you are different from me.
Find someone who is like you
and make your dream come true.

I like apples and you like pears
I hug people and you hug bears.
When I care, you say who cares?
I say its your fault, you say no, it's theirs.
I want to spend holidays in my swimming pool
you say somewhere else it's cool.
You like brunets and blondes, but I am red hair,
the same taste we don't share.
Feelings of love should be the same
We are very different as you can see,
everyone should find their cup of tea.
The world has millions or people,
good luck to you and good luck to me."

BILLIONS OF PEOPLE

Billions of people,
billions of hearts,
billions of dreams,
live every day.

They don't know where to go,
they walk
and of the future they think.

While God sees,
God listens,
God knows everything
but doesn't tell.

THE HUMAN NOVEL

Sad shadows show before me
voices of dead, unseen faces.

The sky's birds condemned me
and cast me off behind the sun.
I was burned and broiled
in the desert exiled.

They beat me while I slept
because I hoped in truth.
But in vain, it was an illusion,
thus, I cry in sorrow.

Hope or something else rare
keeps the human alive,
living in a dream or for real
this only God knows.

We are all part of this history
but there are those
who don't understand strangely!
We walk and walk
without knowing where we go,
without thinking what we were before.

Unkind people,
unjust flatterers,
only gossip and stay.
Women and men cigarettes smoke.
We wait and wait
the fate's hours
and hide without conscious.

Went by this day
very fast we passed it by.
Good and bad
what did we win?

This silent night
sleeps with open eyes.
These stars how they stand?
Tell me where are they caught?

Oh, how much I dream
beyond this world to live,
I want nothing to remember anymore,
volcanoes of thoughts
want to strangle me.

Leave me, leave me in calm
that my fragile heart can work like a clock.

Go by the days, months, years,
a new generation comes
another dies away.

And comes a moment
when man dies,
thus, it is the moment that man goes
his body as a candle fades away.

Important is what happens after.
Does his spirit remain alive?
Has he done good or no?
Has he gone away from darkness?

Indeed we live in a time of madness
but which one is your role people?

The human novel
is continuing to be written,
in minds and in books
always will be saved.

The human as a virtual being
shouldn't make fatal mistakes.
Run and run the sins of the human being,
now has remained
only the thread of the candle.

If we had more wisdom
if we lived with love,
we would deserve the word "human".

www.ingramcontent.com/pod-product-compliance
Lightning Source LLC
Chambersburg PA
CBHW051103160426
43193CB00010B/1296